Hidd

Hidden Gems

Moonsoulchild

Hidden Gems

Hidden Gems

Copyright © Sara Sheehan

All Rights Reserved

ISBN: 9798832457505

Hidden Gems

Hidden Gems

Hidden Gems is a perspective, it's the literal gem that is my *heart* and *soul*. It's easy to relate to something when it's close to what you're going through, and it could be uncomfortable to read something when you're not ready to hear or heal from it. Sometimes you just want to bask in the feeling of exactly what you're feeling. Each page is set to a certain tone and emotion. This is a warning, there may be emotions, memories, and wounds you might not want to open. I hope you find yourself within this Gem and you see your growth too. Lastly, let me take you down my journey.

Hidden Gems

Hidden Gems

Intro

I'm sorry if my work may trigger you, but ultimately, it's the hard truth so many are not willing to accept or ready for. Read it when you're ready, don't tell me I'm wrong or argue with me about it. I lived it. I almost broke myself trying to rewrite it. I understand it can be a sensitive topic. I know it's not easy. When someone finds themselves in my work, I find it comforting. A safe space, knowing we're never alone. We all go through something similar but still incredibly different. Sometimes my work isn't for everyone, I've accepted that too. Not everyone is at the same place in their journey as I was in those moments I'm reflecting on. I'm sharing my truth because I know there's someone out there that needs some healing, and my work may be the compass they need.

Hidden Gems

Hidden Gems

A message to my trauma:

I said my goodbyes to the things I couldn't keep holding onto. I was tired of letting you tear me apart. I was exhausted trying to find ways to fill voids through souls knowing I could never build homes within broken walls and improper foundations. I was searching for someone to heal me, but the bandage never stuck. I wasn't aware I had to be my own redemption. I felt hollow, echoed by sadness, and hidden in spaces I couldn't seek comfort. I created a bond with trauma, I became codependent on getting my heart broken. I became reckless with my heart when I held it hostage from growth. I thought since someone broke me, they deserved to compensate me for my loss. It was a messy game I played to be loved. I thrived in sadness; it was the only feeling that wasn't fleeting.

Moonchild

I want to be like the moon, beautiful no matter what phase I'm in. I want to shine in my darkest hour. I want to remain a mystery but leave you with enough emotional depth. I want you to feel different after connecting with me- to always remember me. I want you to escape to me when in need of refuge, so I can remind you, even when idle you hold great purpose.

Hidden Gems

Transparent love

I want to thank you for loving me, even if it wasn't enough or the way I deserved. I needed your love, as intangible as it was, it brought tranquility before the storm. It helped me adore myself more. It highlighted the compassion I was lacking for myself. I was devoted to you, blindly stubborn… I was unstable and cruel to my own heart. It was almost like you were a sad song, one I kept overplaying because it ignited something in me… until you sucked all the tenderness out of me. I no longer wish to hit replay.

Hidden Gems

Heart to Hearts with my Inner child

I promised you I would never dig up what I made peace with, that once I healed from it I wouldn't let it harass me into being an afterthought. I knew the cost of dredging up the delicate moments but reflecting was better than suppressing. I know you felt like revisiting those broken moments would only revive those fires that couldn't be tamed. I know you felt I would sink back into that dark place. I know parts of you still live there. I want you to know I'm sorry, for dragging you through the misery like a bad song on repeat. I want you to know, that I always heard you, I just wasn't ready to listen. I want to apologize for neglecting you while I searched for ways to free myself, I should have catered to you, too. I ran from you instead of embracing you. I thought the trauma that surrounded my heart was me surviving my karma. I should have trusted you.

Hidden Gems

Censor

Overindulgence with shame, I constantly persuaded myself to silence my rage. I looked in the mirror and saw every opinion I digested and every flaw that never went undetected. I highlighted my imperfections. I rehearsed being rejected. I felt unseen, distorted, and out of place. I couldn't see past the judgments, the insecurities, and now the picture I painted myself to be. I was influenced by the persona of me through the eyes of others. I was never discovered or loved for the essence of who I was. I was told who I was before I could find myself. I was judged by my flaws before I could embrace them, which is why I spent half of my life trying to erase them.

Hidden Gems

2.22.22

I promise to always stay true to my authentic self. To stay in touch with my intuition, to listen and let it guide me. I will never let go of my desire to keep living my wildest dreams. I will keep loving hard. I will believe in my magic. I will always give myself the flowers I deserve, I won't wait for anyone to give them to me. I will give them to those who deserve them too. I promise to love everyone close, to never make them feel small or ever question my love. I won't wait until they're dead and gone, I will always shower them with love, support, and security. I will never feel threatened if their success is ahead of mine, I will always be proud. I will be present in every moment. I won't let anxiety riddle me. I won't let depression suffocate me. I won't let the past come back to haunt me. I keep my word to no longer nurture dead things. I understand what's taken from me was the transition I needed to become my highest self. I had to prioritize my healing. I

Hidden Gems

had to dive deep into the depths of my soul to heal my inner child. I had to be uncomfortable to grow. I vowed to never let the dark times cloud the light, like the moon, finding my beauty within in the darkness and the madness.

Sometimes I feel uneasy. Sometimes I feel powerful. I know the shift in my emotions will always be temporary. I forgive myself for putting so much pressure on feeling guilty because I never was where I wanted to be. I had a higher purpose. To manifest is one thing, but I learned wishing does nothing without work. These days, I look at the bigger picture. I'm here and there's always room to rewrite my story. You'll never catch me missing old versions of who I was, I have no shame. These days I love myself more.

Finding Solitude

I once thought love was the cure for loneliness until I fell in love with someone who made me feel lonely. Love betrayed me… everything I once believed love to be traumatized me. The canvas I perfected was ruined, completely shattered into this heartbreaking memory of PTSD. The mirror of my pain was a reflection of sharing the same moment with someone else. I was terrified to give myself to anyone because of my deep fear of being abandoned. I was left soaking in my shadow of despair until I realized my greatest epiphany, there was no love so fulfilling, and there was no one so rare, who could cure me. I was looking for love in all the wrong places. I was expecting someone to love the broken version of me because I couldn't.

Hypophrenia

The tug of sadness that comes to haunt and hug me tight, leaving me blue… comes without a purpose. The tears flow silently while my anxious nerves don't get a second to rest. To be sad without a source, I never suffered more- feeling hopeless and worthless. At least when it's targeted I could feel something. I never liked feeling numb.

Hidden Gems

I'm not a *pitstop*
kind of love,
my heart is the destination.

Hidden Gems

Healer

I once felt entitled to someone, like I was obligated to forever have a place in their life because I was a source of healing for them. I was convinced I deserved more than being a healer to someone who ended up bringing me to my darkest hour. I felt used when they left me as if they used my love to form a weapon against me. Like they took my love and used it to love someone else. I didn't realize we outgrew each other, and they never owed me anything. I gave them a piece of myself, I let them in and I loved them, none of this was against my will. It was a lesson, a piece of myself I needed to learn to meet the healed version of myself.

Hidden Gems

Apology I deserve to give myself

The one thing I always hoped was that you'd find someone worthy of you. I forgot to tell you it wasn't your job to make them see, maybe if I did you wouldn't have been constantly searching for acceptance and validation from everyone. I taught you to find comfort and make a home there, but I didn't tell you that even comfort can be misleading, maybe then you would have protected your soul from intruders who sucked the love right out of you. I taught you to fight for love, only if I would have known the definition, I could have saved you from that cheap version and so much heartache and that easily forgiving habit you formed. The pattern of overthinking to the point you accepted the lowest form of love. You allowed jealousy; manipulation, gaslighting, and abuse as a form of love. You spent your whole life living outside

Hidden Gems

your comfort zone. You let people criticize you without standing up for the idea of who you thought of yourself to be. You weren't strong enough- you were fragile, living in a glass house. You were fighting the monster in you. Surviving that layer of you was the hardest battle, but you handled it with so much grace. You are no longer fragile, you're whole. You are everything you said you were. The journey is beautiful. I'm so happy you're free.

Hidden Gems

I wore my heart
on my sleeve
like it was an open invitation
to break me.

Hidden Gems

Don't use "love" as an excuse to keep unwanted company around your soul. Don't use "love" as an excuse to fight for a connection that's outgrown you. Don't use "love" as an excuse to rebuild bonds that bandages never stuck to, the wound is still fresh. Don't use "love" as an excuse to be a doormat to someone who carelessly "missteps" and "doesn't mean to hurt you". Don't use "love" as an excuse to stay, when the only love you're fighting for is the love you're giving that was never returned. Don't keep accepting that form of love or you'll forever be a stranger to your own heart.

Hidden Gems

Let the dust settle

The past is a dangerous place. A route that is often taken when you're feeling insecure in your current state. To reminisce can be a dreamy place. It can bring chaos into a place of solace. Asking someone to dig up their ghosts and unleash their demons can be a terrifying ride. Asking someone to recall moments and mistakes can cause them to shut down. If you aren't ready to accept them for everything that pieced them into the soul they came to love, don't take that turn. Don't let someone be vulnerable with you just to leave them stranded. It takes a lot of courage to put your heart on the line. You got the truth when they could have lied, but they decided to be transparent. Allow them to stand in their truth, that kind of love stands the test of time.

Hidden Gems

To Innerstand

I was once lost,
I hurt good people
because of my unhealed trauma.
I had pure intentions
that went tainted when I
felt insecure or felt I wasn't enough.
It was all in my head.
I had to heal alone,
no one could do that for me.

Hidden Gems

Be with someone who is as transparent as you, someone who communicates through and doesn't ghost when they're upset, but also respects the boundaries of space needed to clear one's mental space. Someone who loves every fiber of your being. Someone who takes the time to listen without reacting. Someone who lets you reflect without judgment. Someone who supports without expecting the same effort, they do it because they believe in you. Someone who is effortlessly your chosen safe place. Someone who doesn't fear your past but takes the time to learn the broken parts of you, without the need to repair… but never repeats those patterns with you. Someone who loves you because of every imperfection. Be with someone who makes it easy to love them, after feeling so hard to love. I think everyone deserves to find that one person who makes all the difference.

I think everyone deserves a healthy love.

Hidden Gems

People swear a healthy love is nonexistent. That someone loyal, doesn't judge and listens to you is hard to find. That someone who doesn't use your past against you, but instead uses it to learn you, to never repeat those patterns, is a fairytale. That someone who feels like home is out of reach. That someone who believes in you supports you and loves every fiber of your being is just a figment of your imagination. A healthy love exists. All these things exist. To believe you will find this healthy love is one thing, but you will never believe you'll find it if you're not this healthy love. Until you realize your worth, you'll keep accepting love with unhealthy patterns. **The love you find will always be a reflection of you**.

Hidden Gems

Temporary love

I never loved the same way twice. To inner stand, this took a lot of digging and forgiveness. It took a lot of acknowledging I wasn't always the victim, but it also wasn't always my love that was tainted. I vowed to never love the same once my heart was abandoned and evaded misery. I was transparent to the heartbreak; I knew the only cure would be to find a harmony in tune… repeating the same old song would only bring a melody of chaos and symbolize how broken I would always end up. Loving the same would only burden me, I couldn't keep letting everyone get the best parts of me. Everyone who ignited a fire in me didn't deserve to be my endgame, some were only a flame.

Hidden Gems

What I wish I could have said to my broken self:

You will make it through. The storm is only passing by. The lessons will translate perfectly. Don't resent the journey. This rebirth will only cause a bit of discomfort- so please, don't settle for a comfortable moment you've been subconsciously trying to outgrow. Healing doesn't mean a clean slate. Healing is a purge to finally silence the demons. Healing is regrouping your innocence. Healing isn't forgetting- it's accepting and creating a different story with a different mindset. Protect your heart from souls who bring darkness with them, they will only be a disservice to you. Disconnect from anyone who robs you of your tenderness. Don't build homes in souls who need saving, you will only mourn them while trying to save yourself. Real strength is through the moments you feel broken- there's always a moment of peace. The darkest moments hold the most light. Don't

Hidden Gems

ever surrender, there's always time to rewrite. Feel free to escape when you need space. Never punish yourself for feeling- your vulnerability is the essence of your being. You aren't defined by their reviews of you. Always be transparent, accountable, and honest- but don't compensate for those who are afraid to love you. If only you could meet the healed version of yourself and see what I always believed.
Embody your magic.

Unstable lover

I was pushy when it came to affection, anytime someone got close, I over-loved. I had this sense of entitlement because of my tender heart, I didn't think I deserved to be done wrong. I had no doubt I was worthy of being loved. I was messy… I latched myself to anyone who opened the floodgates of my heart. I believed the disguises. I had the desire to write the story of forever- a masterpiece written in the stars. I was clingy. My toxic habit became a pattern, my love became tainted. I became the unstable lover I tried so desperately to escape.

Hidden Gems

Tragedy

Loving the idea of someone
without innerstanding them,
will only leave you empty.
Heal the broken parts of you,
before you
devote what you can't embrace.

- *don't leave them broken too*

Hidden Gems

Illusions

We all have loved someone who ended up not being who they portrayed. They got us to that vulnerable place and used it to manipulate us, so much so, we lost ourselves within them because of our need to rescue. We forgot about us. We fell in love with who they pretended to be.

Hidden Gems

No one meant for me
ever came
twice in this lifetime.

Hidden Gems

Our time has expired
Our love will always remain.
Some bonds don't break,
Some are meant to fade.

- *we couldn't promise fate*

Insomnia

It's like all my thoughts meet up to have a conversation when the clock hits rest. I look over and it's 2 a.m. and here I am, thinking of every possible scenario in my head. I start to question my subconscious, is this what I've been hiding? Some of my darkest thoughts come as I lay to rest. I get anxious at the thought of not falling into a slumber too quickly, I envy those who do. I'm a day sleeper and a night owl. Sleep and I once had a healthy relationship, now it's like my creative clock keeps me from it.

Hidden Gems

Don't fake it with me,
be brutally honest
even if it ruins me.
Too many times
I've fallen for a fantasy.

My Apologies

I'm sorry I wasn't enough for you, but I tried to be in every way it counts. I'm sorry you couldn't see my gift, my potential until you were threatened by someone who did. I'm sorry you took for granted a heart that was never broken, but a little damaged- which always balanced the scales. I'm sorry you couldn't find yourself so you gaslight your way through me. You broke me down and convinced me I was already broken, so me being the bad guy worked in your favor. You were never good at accountability or communication, which you realized once the clock ran out of time... our time. I'm not sorry about it, it brought me a greater lesson than any heartbreak ever could. How could I be sorry about a love that stayed consistent, a heart unmatched, and a soul yearning? I couldn't... you should be sorry for never cherishing those things.

Hidden Gems

Roots

I started planting this garden
of reassurance,
bliss and fortune.
I wanted to recreate my story,
and somehow transform the narrative.
I was tired of basking in the unfortunate
and the unknown.
I was tired of living in the shadows.
I learned how to grow.

Hidden Gems

Big-hearted

I have no time to be foolish with a passion like mine. I don't have the means to undress your distress. I have no business trying to save you while you empty me, but I will, and I have. My heart beats on a higher frequency- I was created differently. I would rather break my own heart to save you the heartache, I believe that says a lot about the kind of heart I carry.

Hidden Gems

What's love?

Don't be fooled by your version of love, by the love you keep accepting. Gaslighting looks a lot like love. Sometimes your heart is set on being needed. When someone lingers with lust, you have faith love could grow in its place and when it doesn't you still beg it to stay. Love is only scary when you accept its disguises. Love is only scary when you worship the idea of it.

Hidden Gems

No saviors

I never expected someone to rescue me,
even at the times
I needed saving.
I reserved that for myself.
I would never put a burden that heavy
on anyone
just to leave them empty.

Hidden Gems

My Truth

I don't think we talk enough about how uncomfortable "let's move past it, let's move on" is when it comes to something you won't ever forget. It's not wrong to not want to forgive, that maybe we don't wish to dig up what still lingers in our hearts- the mistrust and rage we caged in. I think it's okay to not wish to be numb forever and never escape to that dark place again. I don't think we talk enough about being apologetic doesn't heal you nor does it always bring ease to your weary heart. The memory still wanders the mind. The pain will always resurface throughout your journey, within yourself and the people you come to know. It's become a piece of you, and you can't let it go. Giving someone the privilege of my forgiveness when they don't deserve it would only deepen my wound. The irony, I will heal regardless. The closure is the broken pieces of me. The lessons shaped me. I forgive myself and I will do it without feeling like a hostage.

Wasteland

I took pride in being the healer until I realized I couldn't fix anyone. I could only love them for the version they gave me. I couldn't love them for their potential without breaking my own heart. I couldn't bring out the version of them I wanted to love me. I had to swallow my pride and forgive myself for trying to manipulate someone into loving me through my heart's language, while I used their pain as a weapon because they couldn't love on the same frequency as me.

Hidden Gems

Heartbreak Debt

I never thought anyone could be in love with me. I never thought I held the capacity to be loved. I knew how far I'd go for the idea of love. I knew the depths my heart would go for who I loved, but this maze of love never reciprocated, or somehow fell short. I found myself feeling smaller every time someone left, the investment cost me so much. I just wanted to be loved.

Hidden Gems

I loved you and your heart belonged to someone else. It was wrong for me to try and make you love me, but it was your brokenness that convinced me you may have needed me.

… I thought we could heal each other.

Hidden Gems

I **protect** my heart by reserving my love for those who are worthy.

I **protect** my energy by freeing anything before it consumes me.

I **protect** my aura by stayin' a mystery.

I **protect** my soul by being selective about who gets close to me.

I **protect** my body by supplying more self-love, and more self-care.

I promise to **protect**, to always do right by me... I deserve that kind of stability. I deserve that kind of devotion.

Hidden Gems

My heart was too divine
to keep putting it on display
for those,
who were only fluent
in walking away

- *It was hard getting anyone to stay*

Hidden Gems

Sensitivity

If it's one thing I wish to be remembered for, it's for the souls I touched and left a mark on, even if it was for a fleeting moment. I want to be remembered for the way I love. I always make sure I show up when it's needed and check up when there's some distance. I always make sure everyone I love knows how much they're loved and how much I love them. I think that memory stays the longest.

Hidden Gems

A soulmate tale:

"They stay forever"
Except they always don't.
Sometimes they aren't meant for you
Sometimes they're a lesson
Sometimes the timing could be different.

You never know,
Sometimes it's never,
Sometimes it's forever.

A soulmate is engraved forever in your heart, you will always remember… doesn't mean it's promised forever.

Hidden Gems

Heartbreak Paradox

I was codependent with trauma,
I created this bond with heartbreak.
I thrived in chaos,
I didn't feel purpose without it.
My ideal love
was to heal the hurting,
without it
I was nothing.
Once I healed them,
I served my purpose.
My errors of love
I wrote into my life,
I searched for within the broken.
Once I healed them,
I was left with nothing.

Hidden Gems

Not Feeling Good Enough

I don't think we talk enough about the trauma of not feeling good enough. Never feel like what we give is enough, because we constantly need to always give more to get effort. Never feeling like we are worthy because we chase every chance at being wanted. We don't often talk about the trauma of accepting someone into your life who isn't meant for you after they've shown countless times they're the wrong piece but you try to mold yourself into what they need… because that ounce of what felt like love they gave was enough to cave. We don't talk about the unhealthy yearning of being loved that we'd do anything to feel it, we'd let anyone who brings comfort. We don't talk about how it starts with security and ends with uncertainty. We don't talk about the toxic hold we put on others when we use them to feel something when they're incapable of delivering and we feel damaged. We don't talk about the fear of letting go because we inhale the festering aroma of our gaslighting performer. We fear never feeling the mirage they handled with care again. We don't talk about the burnout and bareness of picking up the pieces, the fear of feeling something real. We don't talk about how the hopeless romantic can lose hope too.

Hidden Gems

Not Good Enough II

We forget to talk about the parts we adopt in these cycles of our hearts abuse and how we form these patterns by not wanting to. My want to feel love, that's on me, but when they take advantage of my fragile heart, that's when the tables turn. Accepting someone in my life when the signs have proven they're not for me, that's on me, but when they use my love as a pawn, that's where the line is drawn. We often blame someone else for the pain we endure, and we forget to take accountability for our part in our heartache. It's true, that we set these expectations for everyone because we want to feel the experience of a soul connection. We're left damaged, sensitive, and guarded when someone tries to walk in after. We don't talk about how we've sacrificed it all for love when it's not love… it's the illusion of what we manipulated ourselves to believe love to be and how dangerous it became to be.

Hidden Gems

Mourning

So much time has passed,
I still think of you.
I still wonder
what we could have been
if I wasn't running from my truth.
I didn't want to ruin you.

- *I ended up broken too*

Hidden Gems

Wanderlust

I let you go, I set you free.
I knew under the circumstances
we'd never love each other
the way we deserved to.
We were both broken,
We were both searching
for something we couldn't match.
We just wanted to feel wanted.
We just wanted to feel **something**.

Hidden Gems

A message from my inner child

You don't need to apologize for neglecting me when I reached out to console you, I understand you were grieving a version of yourself you weren't familiar with. I wasn't going to let you drown in your self-destruction but I tried to comfort you many times through memories and things that could remind you of your gift... but you stayed stuck in your ways and I don't blame you for trying to live without me but it was me who had to wipe those silent tears while you broke every time you overextended your heart to those who weren't worthy. I pondered many times; did you forget me? It was like you disguised yourself- a façade I wasn't fooled by. You were living a life with the only truth told was your desire to show your heart. Without a doubt, you succeeded but always got stuck in the intangible of not being loved in return. I tried guiding you through the dark. I thought my years of knowledge could heal you, but you never listened. It was important for you to learn your lesson and you did but through so much heartbreak. You grew strong and wise, I'm so proud of you.

Hidden Gems

Lessons of Love

I never met someone who didn't love me after knowing me, a touch of my energy sparked those soul ties. It always brought me to those who were timid to love. I also attracted those who were broken, mending, and vindictive. Not everyone had the same intentions I had. Not everyone who loved me respected me, and deciphering the two took a lot of learning. The toughest lesson was trying to understand not everyone who loved me was ready for my love.

Hidden Gems

I was always worthy,
I just put my purpose
In the wrong hands.

My love was never tainted-
I just *invested* in the **wrong hearts**.

Hidden Gems

My heart was the gift

I lost my emotional stability trying to free them from their madness. Without the need to save them, there wasn't anything holding me there, as I attached myself to the idea they were treasure. I searched for the key to unlock the hidden gift deep inside them. You see, I became blinded by the game. I focused on the main issue, they needed love too. I made it my mission to win, to give them everything they were never given. I created this façade of who I envisioned them to be... the someone I always wished to love me. When the idea started to fade, I realized it was my love, energy, and vulnerability that was the gift. When the infatuation of them being the home I subconsciously built, the one I nourished that they left unfinished. The bruise they left on my heart. I was left evicted from the safe place I once had in mind. Once I unlocked the treasure, I started to unravel the toxic cycle. They were a different kind of gift, a stone-cold deception- someone who wasn't worthy of my love.

Keep the faith

I've been damaged,
fragile and unsteady.
I never rehearsed my brokenness,
I never changed my heart.
I was in desperate need to feel,
I knew even the darkest souls
could be loved.

- *some are reckless with their hearts*

Hidden Gems

Pardon

Forgiveness isn't a clean slate. Forgiveness is accepting someone's truth and trusting them to stand in it. Forgiveness is opening your heart to someone after they left you with so much damage. It takes a lot of courage to ask for forgiveness especially after bringing sorrow. It takes a lot of fearlessness to be the one to forgive. You forgive but you never disremember. It's something that lives with you forever. You need to be at a place in your life to know that being perfect is an illusion, mistakes are bound to happen. It's up to you to choose where it leads you and how heavy the burden is to carry. Forgiveness isn't just accepting an I'm sorry, it's letting someone have the chance to demolish you, not once, but twice.

Hidden Gems

Narcissist Reflections

A narcissist will suck you for every good you have in you, they will convince you that you're no good… it's true. They will also have you questioning yourself and you end up developing toxic traits, you become right where they want you. When you free yourself from the hold they have over you, it's up to you to put in the work to heal and unlearn those patterns they placed on you. Letting yourself escape the pain and trauma will keep you in that dark place subconsciously, you won't see it but you will repeat these behaviors to everyone who comes in after. There's no such thing as a distraction for healing, you suppress and become a toxic risk to your mental health and everyone who loves you. It's not about finding love with someone opposite of what you've loved before… it's about healing the version of you that holds the trauma and pain that attracts the wrong ones. There's a difference between being trauma bonded with someone and having a bond with trauma. It's important to look deep inside because it all starts with you. If you forever run from the demons that haunt you, you will forever accept the love that only hurts you.

Hidden Gems

Gentle heart,
don't lose your tenderness
pretending to be cold

- *you won't find what you deserve*

Hidden Gems

Advice for creatives

Whatever you pursue, make it you. Don't dim or hide who you are… express yourself completely in your art. Masterpieces aren't made without the darkest moments so don't be ashamed of who you once were, who you will become when you stand in your truth will free you. Living in the persona of who they created you to be will only confuse you. Don't be afraid to stand out, fitting in will only keep you hostage from your potential. Don't settle for anything you wouldn't want to live in forever. Don't overcompensate your energy for it to be matched, align your purpose and you won't feel attacked. As a creative, you feel everything deeply, more than a lot of people you will come across… embrace that, and don't worry about the ones who won't feel you.

Hidden Gems

The Battlefield

I was pushy when it came to love, and storms of doubt flooded my self-worth. I broke down to open myself to anyone if there was a chance I was going to be loved. The root of my entitlement was my soft heart. I was a nurturer, so a broken heart was a match for my savior complex. My purpose was to fix and heal. Too often I was left empty after each repair. I was giving but never receiving, it never seemed fair but I never seemed to care. I was hoping my love would win some over but my big heart was overlooked, I couldn't blame anyone but myself. I was letting myself get taken for granted while giving the best parts of me to someone who couldn't handle them, let alone keep them safe.

Withdraw

I use to question the absence of the ones who departed from my life. The nostalgia of our love held me tight. I didn't have the transparency to see that maybe they weren't meant for me. I was convinced once I loved them, it was forever. I wasn't aware growth would come in and change my direction. I held onto the good in them and tried to create a version of them that was for me. These days, I let them go, I appreciate the joy they showered me with, and embrace their departure. Some souls aren't meant to ride with me through every moment of my journey, it wasn't up to me to decide, or to fight it. Knowing they served their purpose and I did mine was enough for me.

Hidden Gems

Love Language

I'm not going to agree with everything for the sake of your pride. I'm going to be honest with you, even when it hurts.

Honorable

The right people will always stand by you, they will always stay. It's no question if they should or whether it's healthy for them, they were always going to stay. When an honest soul loves you, it can be dangerous for them, because they will overlove. When someone honorable loves you, they will always compensate for the vacant parts of you- they don't ever want to see you hurting. We all are capable of being the right person, we just need to stop catering to the hopeless so gracefully. We just need to stop investing in souls who don't have what we need to offer, and not try and make them, or led them on.

Hidden Gems

Sonder

I can't take back how I felt all these years because my feelings are valid. You ghosting and coming back without a reason left a bruise on my heart, one that won't ever fade. I wondered for years whether I wasn't enough or who it was that ran you away. I need to live without getting answers to my questions, and I'm at peace with living without that piece of me. Parts of you were a mystery, you were good at stayin' low. That emptiness in me turned to anger, one that was brewing in me for so long. I didn't once consider you could be projecting because of your demons. I know it's more complex than just the truth being told. You would need to dig deep and unleash those dark memories you wished to forget. You would need to release emotions you shut off from, some so, were the reason you left. You would need to face everything again, after reliving it and also running from it your whole life. I tried to think of every scenario because I thought it would hurt less, but the truth left me emptier. I guess we'll always be bonded by trauma- you eluding your demons, and me, paying for them.

Hidden Gems

Turn the page

Closure is important if you feel the need to obtain it but sometimes it does nothing to help the grief that's hovering over you. Sometimes you're left wondering and you need to accept sometimes you'll never know why but find peace in the unknown. Sometimes when I feel my lowest I try to remind myself of the good that I am, the heart I behold, and the potential I have to become. It's easy to cater to the sadness. It's harder to heal it. It will hurt a lot before it feels good. There's always a bigger picture, a bigger purpose… make sure you always make time to appreciate the things still growing and not just the loss. You will never learn to swim if you continue to let yourself drown in heartache. Make something beautiful from it.

Hidden Gems

A Pick Me

Nothing brings the heart more turmoil than the need to be chosen. The yearning to be desired. The thrill of that fleeting moment and the constant chase to feel it again. Developing a bond with desire from the trauma of never feeling good enough. Nothing brings the soul more loss than the need to be found. The need to be felt. The need to be heard. Holding onto people after they let you go will only burden you. Heal the broken parts of you before you search to fill a void only you were meant to fulfill. You deserve so much more than to feel chosen by someone who can't choose themselves first. Don't give someone that much sway, you will always be chosen the wrong way.

Hidden Gems

Your departure
wasn't what broke me
It was trying to love myself
after only loving you.
It was trying to separate
the reality of the fear
of never being good enough.

Hidden Gems

Versions of love

I've been loved in many ways. I've been loved by someone who couldn't hear me when I spoke my potential. I've been loved by someone who couldn't support what they couldn't understand because of their lack of passion. I've been loved by someone who couldn't feel me but used my love as a strength for them to thrive. I've been loved by someone who highlighted my insecurities so they could forget about theirs. I've been loved by someone who dimmed down my light, who made me believe I was the darkness. I've been loved by someone who made me believe my heart didn't deserve a rare love. I've been loved by someone who took me to that euphoric place just to leave me stranded. I've been loved by someone who used my love as a weapon against me. I've been loved by someone whose first language was to lie. I've been loved by someone who didn't feel like I was enough. I've been loved by someone who inspired me, stood by me, and made sure I was aware I was worthy. I've been loved by someone who made me feel safe. I've been loved by someone who never made me feel small or tried to convince me I wasn't deserving. I've been loved by someone worthy, someone worth giving my all to. I've been loved by someone who never forgot to remind me how imperfect love may be, but it only feels out of reach when you give it to the wrong ones. I've been loved in many ways, by many different souls but it's the way I love myself that sets the love that finds me in place, because I, have also loved myself in all these ways.

Hidden Gems

Wake up call

Self-love was a tale I often never told.
It was a script I rewrote until I believed it to be true. I didn't know who I was, I was lost until I discovered comfort. It helped distract me from the parts of me that were broken. It helped me open my eyes to the parts of me that needed to heal.

Hidden Gems

Mirror Talks

I accept you for everything that made you who you are and shaped you into this beautiful being. I accept the gap that makes you unique. I accept the acne and the scars, they don't make you less of who you are. I embrace the changes in your body. I accept your little tummy after years of running from being "too thin"… I accept finally feeling safe in my skin.

Hidden Gems

I owe myself an apology
for allowing fear and rejection
to make a monster out of me.

The Narcissist

To be in love with a narcissist is a slippery slope. It's a dangerous place to be, especially since you're unaware of the tendencies because you're blinded by your love for them, and the good they once portrayed. A narcissist is someone who believes they're superior, someone who deserves to call the shots… someone who loves themselves a little too much. What we rarely talk about is how a narcissist isn't superior, they're extremely insecure, and they strive to control you until the narrative plays in their favor. A narcissist will find someone who they can weaken, someone who is unaware of their worth… someone who they can dig deep enough to pull the strings. You see, a narcissist will be someone you admire, someone you will fall completely in love with because of their will to make you feel something because their acting skills are unmatched. A narcissist will get you where they want you and use you as a tool to make themselves feel better and they'll do this by making you question

Hidden Gems

your worth. They'll flip the script and blame you for every scandal they played a part in, somehow making you believe it was your fault. They'll take you away from everything you once loved to cater to their need and their fear of being alone. They'll have you forgetting who you are because you're so far into trying to save them from themselves. We don't talk enough about how a narcissist will never love you more than they love to control you. We don't talk about how a narcissist rarely loves you at all… they're just trying to love themselves by controlling you. Lastly, we don't talk enough about how you can't save a narcissist… you will just fall deeper into the slump of their possession, their hypnosis of love they convinced you to believe to be real.

You deserve

You deserve a love that doesn't force you to leave behind the things and people you love. You deserve a love that comes with conditions but is based on the foundation and boundaries you set. You deserve a love that isn't belittling, that never makes you question or lose your worth. You deserve a love that finds and embraces you. A love you don't need to save or make excuses for. You deserve a love that comes with no ulterior motives.

Noxious

I brainwashed myself to believe fighting for someone I loved meant giving endless second chances. I thought another chance meant a clean slate to return to where we left off before pain stepped in. The damage stained. My heart was a revolving door to finding empathy in souls who I had to teach to love me, and who I found temporary homes in. It was the hopeless romantic in me who believed in the countless chances, the wrong timing, and the forever I painted would manifest into what I wanted. I was blinded by what I needed and what life was showing me. I developed my first toxic trait… using manipulation as a form of love.

Hidden Gems

The toxic cycle

One we know too well, we seem to normalize when it shouldn't be. I think it's because we don't talk enough about the unspoken truths in every part of the story, we just talk about our pain and run with it. We don't talk about the constant circle we end up in when we're begging them to understand our love when it's not us that needs to be forgiven, but we make it our mission to be. We don't talk about the marathons we run to try and keep up with the fantasy we placed. We don't talk about the excuses we make for "love" when there's none involved, just the love we feel, even then, it doesn't seem real. We don't talk about the fact love doesn't conquer all and sometimes it hurts, only because we confuse it with pain. We become toxic to ourselves by letting them dive deeper and take a new piece of us with them every time they puncture the wound that never seems to heal. We tend to place ourselves in the mirror of deception, taking the blame for everything that destroyed us to accept them as who we thought of them to be, not the character they presented constantly. The toxic cycle of trying to make someone understand you're a beautiful soul, but they hold no capacity because they don't see themselves that way.

Hidden Gems

Silver Lining

Once I opened my eyes and saw everything clear, I refused to let anyone make me believe love was tainted because of their need to manipulate me to make them feel something, knowing they weren't worthy of anything beautiful I had to give. I started to appreciate myself more when I decided to love them less. I started to take back my power when I realized they were powerless without my permission to gaslight. I chased and fought ways to make it work when I should have never given them a reason to use me, bruise me, and treat me as if I wasn't worthy. Goodbyes were liberating, there was so much freedom in reclaiming what was taken from me. The past has no place in my heart, and neither does the abuser who took my soul for a terrifying ride. The war is finally over, I conquered.

Hidden Gems

Lessons of Love II

What a shame,
to give your heart to someone
and they abandon it.

What a shame,
to adapt to a love
so completely far from the real.

Hidden Gems

The Manipulator

Something we don't often talk about is the wanting of love and once we find it, it seems nothing like we thought it would be. We don't talk about the idea we place on love and try to make everyone feel our love. We don't talk about how it becomes full because we were obsessed with the chase-the wanting to feel the love we forget the meaning of it. We don't talk about having someone good and letting them slip through our fingers because we don't know how to accept someone who's like home, because we never had anyone make us feel that safe. We don't talk about the trust issues and PTSD we're left with from past flames that burnt us out too soon. We don't talk about how we accustom ourselves to believe love was something attached to pain, something we needed to work overtime to attain. We all know the battle of searching for love and always coming up short. We all know the battle of chasing and fighting for love within someone who only brought a storm we couldn't overcome. We

Hidden Gems

all know the story of choosing toxic connections because they're all we know because we broke every good connection that found us. We don't talk about how incredibly toxic we become to ourselves and every one after. We don't talk about the love we lack within ourselves because we neglect ourselves to attain a love that never will exist without knowing our worth. It's a cycle that will repeat until we set the foundation, and boundaries, and know what we deserve. We don't talk about how we will always settle for less than we deserve because we don't believe we deserve something- because someone who wasn't meant for us, because someone we chased and manipulated to love us. We don't talk enough about how a lot of time has nothing to do with our heartache, how it's us and our obsession with wanting love so bad, but not knowing how to love ourselves first.

Hidden Gems

The Gaslighter

One thing we never talk about is the unhealthy attachment to someone who has brought us misery. We don't talk about why because it would be too much to bear, and too embarrassing to speak out loud. We talk about the shattered parts of our hearts and the pain we're left with, but never why we go back and the unhinged patterns we keep letting repeat, refusing to stop the cycle because the same one who brought us that agony also once brought us that softness. We don't talk about wanting to be set free but also wanting to be consoled by the same one who unleashed so much strain on our hearts. Why is it that we latch onto the unstable when we have a choice? I think it's because we invested so much of ourselves into letting them in, that part of us we don't let anyone feel, let alone see… that part of us that's so intimate we didn't know was possible to feel… so we fight to keep it because losing it has played it in our mind on rewind too many times. We've thought of every possible scenario that could go

Hidden Gems

wrong and none ended with them completely crushing our hearts. We've thought of every possible way we could screw it up, how we would be the one to blame… and this is because we never loved ourselves enough to believe we were worthy of a love that's soft and kind, we had no idea what love was so, of course, we would accept the bare minimum. We had no idea what a good partner was because we didn't know how to be one, so the only way we knew how… was to fight, be manipulated, gaslighted, and broken down. We believed love to be all of these things without truly understanding the meaning. We created our definition of what love was and that's why it was so incredibly difficult to part ways with our first mistake. We don't talk enough about how every piece of us we lost within them was a piece of us we didn't need back… it was the piece we let go with them so we could heal and never feel the need to share those same beliefs of love, to never get comfortable with someone who makes us question our sanity.

Hidden Gems

Someone who brings you solace,
someone who brings you pain
they're never the same person.
We don't talk about
the only thing we were chasing
was a fantasy,
an old version
of an outgrown reality.

Hidden Gems

The Impostor

A mirage most of us have been in is the one where you fall for someone good at faking. Someone who doesn't know what they want but want you until they don't, until they feel something better comes along... or someone they let gets away. We don't talk about how uncomfortable it is to want someone who doesn't want us but makes us believe they do, and we end up broken and fighting to hold together a connection that was only felt by us. We don't talk enough about how someone will use you for their needs but completely put yours on do not disturb, ignoring the fact you're capable of feeling, loving, and hurting. We don't talk about feeling completely unstable because of someone who stayed with us for years but walked away one day out of the blue because "it wasn't working" but never communicated it through. We don't talk about overlooking the signs when they're clear in front of us, but we choose to believe the illusion we so desperately wanted to believe. I was never able to wrap my head around how someone could lead you on... make you feel loved, but back away when things start to get serious. I was never able to understand why the fear of a title made some

Hidden Gems

run the other way. The thought of a relationship made them unsettled, to the point they leave you stranded but ended up back with their ex. We don't talk about someone that comes into your life just to ruin you for the next one. We don't talk about how our hearts are completely shattered because this person made us believe in things, we didn't know were possible, just to have us broken for years to come... scared to get destroyed all over again. We don't talk about how this person can come back and spark the same fire and pick up right where we left off and we'd let them because the comfort they brought was something we haven't felt since. We latch to the past because we can't seem to unfeel it and sometimes we don't want to forget it- so we go back and give every piece of ourselves to them, even in the most intimate way because they made us feel loved, in some twisted way we believed the passion made us feel loved not knowing it was just an escape for them until they found something new. We don't talk about how we continue to let ourselves be used and having the ability to walk away as someone new with all the lessons and scars... to never repeat this love we were taught and the patterns we developed along the way. We don't talk about breaking the cycle of the past and never letting them back in.

Hidden Gems

Love never lived
in the same place abuse did.
Your heart is a safe place,
protect it.
There are too many con artists
out here
to give it to everyone
so gracefully.

Hidden Gems

Philophobic

The unspoken truth about getting our hopes up and our idea of romance ruined, all because of someone who led you to the feeling but left you stranded when love because involved. Someone who acts the part until they no longer wish to play the part when titles became involved. We don't talk about how much nurturing we end up doing trying to make the connection stay synced. The lengths, depths, and mazes we go through to save something we never had. We don't talk about the transition of falling for someone to missing old versions of them when we're suddenly presented with their departure from our hearts. We don't talk about the excuses we make when they present their truth. We don't talk about how selfish we are when they present who they are, and we try to convince them otherwise. We believed in what we felt, and our hearts took us to a place we've never been… only to discover it's not reciprocated. We don't talk enough about how it's our worst nightmare having to part ways with our "almost" love… knowing there wasn't anything we could do to make a fleeting moment indefinite.

Hidden Gems

Some *heartbreaks*
you never truly recover from.
You will heal,
and you will move on.
It will just **linger** in your heart forever.

Hidden Gems

Saudade

We don't talk about the codependency we place on someone when we wait, or how extremely unhealthy it is to even wait at all. We all loved someone who didn't want us back. We all placed our hearts all in, giving the best intentions, and ended up with different expectations. We all believed the love we felt was honest, so to go to any length to keep that love was a requirement, even when we got tired we placed the exhaustion to the side to keep fighting for a love that was never for us. We all believed love conquered all, we were never aware that under certain circumstances and conditions it's different. We were never made aware that timing wasn't meant to be tampered with, we had no business trying to force something that wasn't in our path. We don't talk enough about how time is just that… time. Except we saw it as a figment in our imagination and we could make someone love us, or maybe, when they decide to love us we'll be here waiting. We

Hidden Gems

don't talk about sitting on the sidelines watching the one we yearn for, love someone else, and continue to believe that one day it could be us. We don't talk about why we sit and convince ourselves we deserve a love that doesn't deserve us. We don't talk about how unworthy we feel so we try and fill the void with someone new. We don't talk about who we turn down because our heart belongs to someone else. Nothing good comes from waiting. Nothing good comes from forcing or chasing. No one will ever take you seriously when you wait for them, it's like an open door to your heart, they can bruise you and you're still there with all the love to give. You will only be treated exactly how you let yourself be treated. Don't be someone's maybe, someone's "one day". You deserve someone who won't ever make you wait, who never has to question if they care, who will never make you question if they do.

Hidden Gems

Codependent Love

I had an attachment to being needed by someone who wanted to be needed. I craved a connection with those who needed healing. All I ever wanted was to be adored, so I thought maybe if I could prove my love was their cure, in return they could fill me with the love I needed. These attachments led me nowhere but heartbreak.

Hidden Gems

One way love

Unrequited love, the fantasy of love you envisioned, and prayed for but never got to touch. The love that always slipped through your fingers. The love that was never enough, even at the capacity of giving yourself away. We don't talk about how much we try and keep someone like they're a possession and how we blame them for everything once our story is done and the book is closed. We talk about the trauma surrounding our hearts from never receiving anything close to what we gave. We talk about how they manipulated us by leading us on after they told us they wouldn't be good for us- but we don't talk about how we manipulated them to believe they were. We don't talk about how we kept the chapter going until it ran into the next one when we overplayed a storyline that wasn't real. We don't talk about the nights we spent thinking whether to stay or to go and always found an excuse to stay. We don't talk enough about how we make ourselves believe someone loved us and if they didn't, we convinced ourselves they will in time. We talk about how badly we fought for a love that was never honest but never how the signs were always presented and we always overlooked them.

Hidden Gems

Sometimes we love our idea and create it with anyone who shows interest. Sometimes we love hard, too hard, and we fall for anyone who lets us be vulnerable. Sometimes we wish for love and someone shows up and we believe it's a sign. Sometimes someone leads us to a place they convinced us they're the treasure we've been searching for, just to lead us to an unworldly place- a place where we feel we're not worthy to know what true love is because every time we feel it, it's stolen away and we're left to pick up the pieces. We don't talk about how someone leaves us, destroys us, then shows back up again and we assume it's a sign from the universe so we take that second chance. We don't talk about how that second chance was a test and we failed it. We don't talk about how someone can break us and come back and leave again and still be a soulmate. The difference is they were meant to touch you, just not in the same ways you thought. We don't talk about whether the relationship wasn't a relationship or how we begged to keep it. Someone being a soulmate isn't a reason to chase and manipulate them to stay in your life.

Hidden Gems

Soulmate Gospel

We don't talk about how a soulmate can come into your life and make you feel something promising… to demolish it. We don't talk about how sometimes a soulmate is a lesson- a complete rebirth to finding the calm after the storm. The miracle of finding true love, after closing the revolving door of uncertainty. Loving yourself more, you'll never be clumsy with loving the wrong one ever again.

Hidden Gems

Soulmates don't always stay in your life,
but they stay in your heart
for a lifetime.

Hidden Gems

Soulmate lessons

Growing up I thought there was this one person out there. This one person was for me, my soulmate. I searched for this person within everyone I came across, I always came up short. It was because of these quotes and everything that told us that there's one soulmate for us. My outlook on soulmates has changed over the years and I believe we have multiple soulmates and not all are in the form of lovers. Your soulmate can be family, your best friend, or anyone. There are going to be many soulmates who come in and out of your life, but not all are meant to stay. Some will be a lesson; some will be a blessing. Not saying you won't meet a soulmate you will be with forever, because I believe you will. I found mine. People believe they have this one soulmate and there can't be many, but we meet people throughout our lives that we have these crazy connections with and we don't know why and then we can't seem to let them go. It's okay to let people go that we once loved because that love isn't the same, once it turns into pain it's time to walk

Hidden Gems

away. I don't believe true love requires sacrifice because if it was real you wouldn't need to sacrifice anything. Your dreams, the people you love, things you love. the one you love shouldn't ever ask you to change who you are or give up anything you love for them. Soulmates can be around for a moment, month, years, to forever… there's no exact time. They show their purpose and might leave, but it's okay… take what they taught you and cherish them. The one who stays embraces them. Love everyone who comes in and out of your life. It's a beautiful thing to love many souls. Stop searching for that one person within everyone you meet. They will find you, be patient.

Hidden Gems

Not every soul that passes through
will stay in your life,
make sure you learn
what they came to teach you.

Hidden Gems

The unhealed version of you will always attract the hurting. The unhealed version of you will always overlook the good ones. Heal yourself, you will only align with everything for you, your heart, and your soul.

Recovery

Healing starts with placing your energy and everything you once felt into the universe. It's releasing yourself from the patterns, connections, and so much fear. The fear of the unknown and the fear of never feeling something remotely close. Healing is dangerously bittersweet, as it can break you, shape you, and completely mislead you. It's a time when you question the intentions of everyone, including you. Healing tends to open the door to overthinking, overextending, and being overwhelmed. People don't talk about the terrifying parts of healing, which is why people assume healing is peace… then wonder why they haven't made it there. Healing is messy, confusing, and jaded. It's also inspiring, eye-opening, and rebirthing a new you. The situation that ended was meant to, it no longer served you. The love you felt was magnetic and real, there's no doubt about the depth of what you felt or what you feel. There's nothing to say that will undo the pain you're in limbo with. To stay or to go is always the question, but no

Hidden Gems

one talks about when you don't have the option and it's chosen for you. The breakthrough is liberating, but don't resent the journey. There's so much peace in the madness, like when you find out there's something more incredible out there- in you, that you haven't found because you're longing to rebuild, reconnect, and resurrect what's outgrown you. It's cliché, but choose yourself with grace. Honor yourself alone. Finish the unfinished parts of you. Once you find the soul in you, you will drift away from the love you couldn't walk away from. You'll accept the sanctuary that's been awaiting you. The love that chooses you, not the love that makes you chase, save or prove.

Hidden Gems

Breaking free from your trauma is the beginning of another journey. Healing is messy, it's not immediate peace. It's time to unlearn everything you've adapted while holding onto the trauma for so long.

Hidden Gems

We've all been through something heartbreakingly tragic, it's not fair to act like your pain weighs heavier than someone else's just because they healed from theirs. Before you judge someone on their trauma and healing, don't forget the journey it took to find peace.

Chapter 25:
The Healing Process

I can't change the past. I can't change the mistakes. I can't erase the pain. I believe it's not impossible to be only on the end of heartache. There was a time I never brought pain to someone who broke me, if I was ever to blame myself for anything it would be letting them hurt me. I never doubled down and hurt back, my nineteen-year-old self, walked away liberated to never feel that again. Instead, I was a wrecking ball to myself and to many that came after. Maybe it was because I didn't work on myself to heal every broken part, I chose to fill a void that couldn't be filled. I hurt people in the crossfire. I ghosted, I turned into someone I didn't recognize because I was tired of the heartache. I was tired of feeling like I wasn't worthy. I had to forgive myself for it all, to heal. Each story is different- they are never played out the same... breaking them down and analyzing them was an important part of my healing process.

Hidden Gems

A Letter to my Twenties

A journey. You were filled with lessons, loss, and a ton of blessings. A rollercoaster of emotions doing the motions through these 29 years. I started my 20's working a retail job with some great people. I didn't have a plan I was living in the moment. I was trying to make memories and make the most out of my life. I thought I had it all mapped out but where I ended up wasn't my destination. The relationship I was in was something I needed to learn about myself. I was desperately trying to identify myself. I'm thankful for the lessons without them I wouldn't appreciate the blessings. At 24, I had the greatest loss but somehow I grew stronger and wiser through the heartache. Josie, I love you, endlessly. You are an important step in my journey and I will honor our connection and your soul for as long as I'm here. I wouldn't be showing my work publicly without your inspiration. After the greatest loss, turning 25, I published my first book and found my person, the other half of my soul. You are incredible, you are magic. I don't think I can ever thank you enough for the way you

Hidden Gems

love me but I will for the rest of my life. To live my dream with you, someone who shares the same one, our passion is out of this universe. You are a huge inspiration to me.

At 27, I quit my job and became a full-time author, and got blessed with a niece. Here I am, 29. Almost 30,000 books sold since 2018. To this healed and beautiful soul, I've grown to be, I'm so proud for never giving up. I'm so proud of the passion I never let die. I found my gift and I never once looked away from it. At 20 I never would have imagined I'd be here, let alone able to handle growth. My resilience. My magic. My love. Some leave this world without knowing their purpose but I've found mine and it's something I'll never take for granted. To everyone who loves me, I will always cherish your love and support, I love you. To my supporters, thank you for making me feel safe in this place where I share my truth. To everyone who's loved me, thank you for the journey. I learned the journey is more important than the destination, there's never just one. Life is full of them, enjoy each stop.

Hidden Gems

The Real Me

I forgive myself for the times I hid who I was and created a version of myself to be loved. I forgive myself for expecting anyone to love a version of me that was far from the truth. A version that lacked confidence. I couldn't hide my flaws any longer, I had to embrace them. I was looking for love in those who yearned for lust when I should have been looking for those who longed to be loved.

Hidden Gems

Unspoken Truths

One thing we always get wrong is refusing to face our trauma and taking account of everything we've endured before we quickly try and reach the finish line with someone else. I don't think we often talk about the stigma surrounding falling for someone else so quickly after walking away from someone we spent a lot of our lives with, but we often don't talk about how sometimes we left emotionally way before we physically were capable, and there's nothing wrong with that... especially after all the pain we let impact our way of thinking, loving, and growing. When we're in a relationship in the beginning things usually feel like a miracle, we feel as if we finally found a gem we've searched so long for, but once that relationship reaches its time you grow apart and things become unbearable, but you refuse to walk away because times get hard, you were taught to fight for love. What isn't often talked about is that we're never fighting for love, we're fighting for something that's no longer love, something no longer connected to us. No one talks about how it's okay to let go, it's okay to move on. It's okay to know that the love you once felt can't be revived and it's okay to leave it as you once

Hidden Gems

remembered it. No one talks about how it's okay to start over with someone new, even soon after, or if it was calculated when you were emotionally distant from that once-upon-a-time love. There's no rule book to falling and loving... when you find comfort in someone there's no wrong way to do anything.
Never jump into anything when you don't know your intentions, or because you feel lonely, or haven't recovered from the heartache of anything holding pain over you. It is rarely talked about and when it is, it seems cliché, but no one can promise you the world, it's not something that can be given. Putting that much trust in someone will only disappoint you if they leave, as they take the whole world with them you feel worthless. When that **magical** love comes around, they won't need to promise anything, **they will feel like home** and that will be enough.

Hidden Gems

A healthy love will never come from trust issues, old patterns, and suppressed pain. True love will never look into your eyes and lie. Real love will never open your soul without the intention of bringing peace and a place called home.

Hidden Gems

The idea of love

I had lovers who saw the moment
when I saw forever,
It never ended in bliss.
They ended up a ghost,
a shadow of the love I lost.
A faded memory soon extinguished.
If only I didn't rush our forever,
maybe I could have loved
what we had too.

Attachments

I watched someone I adored, love someone else and I thought it was the worst heartbreak I'd ever feel. I developed this attachment to souls who weren't mine, and it broke my heart. I can't blame anyone for my weary heart. I won't apologize for being a hopeless romantic, but I can't blame them for not choosing me. I never thought of myself as a prize anyway.

Hidden Gems

Being an Empath

I tend to fall in love with people who are broken, with a little edge. I tend to fall for people who need to be fixed or reminded of their gifts. I tend to fall for those who need a new chapter, those in need of some healing. I was addicted to being the savior, it gave me purpose.

I only wanted to not feel broken.

Cherophobia

I remember being someone who would fear losing the good in my life. I would overthink every possible scenario that could happen. I didn't know it was the beginning of my self-destruction. The investments, and the effort I poured into everyone's cup drowned me. I put too much in even when I didn't have full trust in place, I just wanted love. I let the wrong ones walk all over me and leave footprints of their cheap potential. I created a war with my heart even when the chaos settled. I didn't believe in anyone's potential because I chose them with my mind closed and heart open. I never trusted my heart because it always led me down the road of disappointment and in this case, destruction. I was living in a disaster of my dangerous thoughts. I was paying debt for all the time I lost choosing the wrong ones. I kept faith I'd find love but destroyed it when it came close. I feared the unknown because I thought controlling the narrative would help me become whole. I no longer fear losing the good because nothing poisonous could destroy me.

Hidden Gems

No reservations

I don't expect anyone to wait for me,
but I do expect them to respect me.
Respect my want for space
and my need for clarity-
I'll get back to you when I'm balanced.
Communication is key,
but so is **patience**.

Hidden Gems

The boundaries I place,
I expect you to respect them.
Don't overwhelm me
into burning bridges
that aren't even finished.

Hidden Gems

3 a.m. Thoughts

I'm not going to argue with anyone about whether this is right or wrong, I do what's best for me always— I protect my heart and my mental health from those who only try to ruin and abuse me. I communicate through, and I give chance after chance… but when something doesn't change and my words didn't seem to help us survive, my presence won't change a thing either. Ghosting is my choice and I've felt so good walking away from people who hurt me intentionally, why would they care about me ghosting them?! Why would they need an explanation? Why do we feel the need to always be right for someone so wrong for us? If you talked it out and gave it another chance and it still didn't work, save your breath… save your sanity, and leave them behind.

Hidden Gems

My Apologies

I'm sorry for ghosting you, even though I felt I communicated as much as I could until I couldn't anymore, that will shadow us forever. I'm sorry I wasn't strong enough to hold us together, nor were you able to save us. I decided what was best for us. I'm sorry I didn't give you the option to unfold your truth one last time. I will live with the missing chapters of your growth, and I know we'll never be what we once were, but this chapter is for growth.

Hidden Gems

Reserved Introvert

My energy is important to me and I learned it's important to not share it with everyone. I keep it safe, not everyone gets the best parts of me. I can read your energy and tell if I vibe with you, that's why it's impossible to break me these days, no one gets close.

Hidden Gems

Unspoken Truth

I don't think we talk enough about the effort we put into the saying "if something is meant for you it will come back to you" and how we once believed it to be true. We don't talk about how we treat it like a fairytale and the ones who once damaged us will somehow rebirth into what we deserve and come back to us. We don't talk about how sometimes someone isn't meant for us. We were made to believe if we let something go and it comes back... it was for us, but we don't talk about it every time they come back it's just another recurring toxic matter. We don't talk about how we never catch a break because we let them back in because we love them, because we somehow convince ourselves the universe planned this. Instead, it was planned to show us to not let old flames burn us twice. We talk about how they hurt us again, but not how we keep letting them. We don't talk enough about breaking the cycle and stop allowing someone who destroyed you a chance at your love again. We don't talk about the reconnection ending up just another heartbreak on our list of regrets.

Burning Bridges

I don't believe anything good comes from rekindling old flames. There was a specific reason it didn't go in your favor. Finding yourself back in the circle of a stimulating past love will ruin you every time. No one talks about how easy it is to go back because you developed a certain comfort with the past. Your expectations start to dim when you keep repeating the same cycle. it's never really acknowledged, whether we go back because of the person or the idea… or our need to feel something. I feel we suppress a different kind of trauma when it comes to settling for the bare minimum of someone because we want them to love us. We make excuse after excuse because we feel like this time will be different. A dozen second chances only to lose them all, to lose ourselves in the end after all. Nothing good comes from opening old wounds, just room for them to cut deeper.

Hidden Gems

<u>Open-minded</u>

I don't judge any situation because I was once too the person who took someone back because I loved them and I believed we could somehow work it out. I don't tell anyone how to heal other than to do it on your time and when you're ready, it's a long journey and sometimes painful... but the outcome is beautiful. I hope you find the love that's meant to blend with you and brings out the best version of you. I hope you find your strength and happiness on the down days and always. Always remember the low days aren't forever, the pain might sting for a little but the love that comes after you let go of the outgrown love will be magical and you'll never question it.

Hidden Gems

Versions of Me

People swear they know you because they once knew you. They forget there are levels, that so much growth has passed and perhaps, they don't know you at all.

Hidden Gems

Break. Heal. Grow

Sometimes there's no other road paved. Sometimes the bridge you built becomes exhausted trying to hold the weight of the constant mistakes. Sometimes you're fragile, damaged, and a raging hopeless romantic. Sometimes there's no taking a moment to breathe. Sometimes there's no right time to say goodbye. Sometimes you need to sacrifice every "what if" and accept what is… sometimes it's time to build a new bridge.

Hidden Gems

A message from my heart

Why do you always choose to stay even after they show you, they're not worthy? Is it because in the beginning, it was wonderful, they did everything they could to win your heart over. It's like they had this secret type of passion when they spoke, the words were enough that actions weren't needed… but were they just good at faking? What was the point in trying to win your heart over? What was the point of making you fall in love with them just to make you confused, for them not to even love you too? It's either you go back because you think there might be a chance that love lives within them and they will somehow learn to love you, or you take them back because they're all you know, and you don't want to start over you don't want to invest love in a completely different soul. You don't think there can be another one, because after all this you don't believe in love anymore. You feel broken and you don't think you can mend yourself back together. The real catch is how you feel isn't forever. You will heal and you will find love again, but you won't find it in the same one who brought you pain. Stop looking back and look forward. Love yourself and you will align with the one.

Hidden Gems

Red Flags

Have you been ignoring the red flags? Have you been ignoring the fact that you've been giving so much of yourself to make them feel loved to make them happy? Do you overlook the time when they make you sad and empty, just to fill them? Do they make you feel like love is a sacrifice, that if they don't like someone you have to give them up, even if you love them? If your dreams are threatening them because they don't have a purpose yet… you need to give up yours. You do these things because you want them to feel happy and you want them to continue to love you. You want them to feel loved, so you do whatever it takes to keep that love. You overlook the pain and the little things that make you upset and sad because you feel it's just a roadblock the universe is throwing at you is a love worth fighting for. This is the

Hidden Gems

problem with red flags they're always overlooked because we're being manipulated to believe we are wrong... that we're doing the right thing by making ourselves dimmed to make the ones we love happy. We overlooked these red flags because we feel like we're doing what we're supposed to do to keep this love honest. We forget this isn't love, it's gaslighting. It's manipulation, it's a false reality we placed on love because we wanted to be loved. Red flags don't feel like red flags, they feel like a sacrifice and that's the problem we have in relationships, we're being controlled. The red flags don't feel like red flags they feel like we're doing what's right because when you're someone that loves to be there, who likes to rescue, save, fix and heal... we realize we can't do any of those things. Those red flags are from the universe to run... but you stayed because you thought you were doing the right thing and that's not wrong at all. You loved them and that love is real to you, them not loving you back is the red flag.

Hidden Gems

I wanted so desperately to fix us,
but we were two souls
bad for each other,
who were only meant to collide.
For a moment
Not forever.
It made me feel something

- *it was no accident*

Hidden Gems

I forgive myself
for giving you so much of me.
You weren't worth losing my worth.
I forgive myself,
for letting you believe you could.

Hidden Gems

My heart doesn't possess evil,
It's incapable of being cold
but don't take advantage
you will regret coming close.

Hidden Gems

Loving someone and being loyal is completely different. You can love someone and do them wrong, especially coming from a place where you're not sure about what you want and who you are.

Love isn't a choice,
loyalty and honesty are.

Hidden Gems

Honesty

I don't believe once a cheater always a cheater. I believe people cheat for a reason and it was calculated. I cheated once, many years ago, because I was fed this version of love and lied to. They told someone they didn't desire me to get them. Someone committing to you while telling someone else the opposite. Being the unidentified and insecure version of myself, I spiraled. I thought hurting them how they hurt me would balance the scales. The way my heart set to love, was crushed, and I only hurt myself. For them, I felt no remorse. To feed me a version of love they didn't intend to give me but kept me around. It would have been best to walk away, but this one mistake I made taught me to never stay with someone who didn't desire or have plans to do right by me.

I don't condone cheating, especially when it comes from a place of enjoyment and doing it for the thrill. I do condone making a mistake and learning from it.
Sometimes we do things from an unhealed place because our morals were misplaced. Sometimes we do things from a place of hurt and we forget we could have saved ourselves so much pain if we walked away.

Hidden Gems

The *insecure* version of myself let this pain fester into years of disappointment and allowed me to let people walk all over me. I cheated once, but they were never loyal. The difference was that I was always honest about it, they could never admit to it.

The **healed** version of myself is all about honesty, freeing my truth, and letting my partner know what the unidentified version of me made the mistake of doing. The difference is, being with someone who values you will never have to question your intentions- you do right by them always.

It doesn't matter if it wasn't cheating, it could have been a mistake of any kind that came to fester and made you do something questionable. I didn't know how to communicate. I let rage and fear take control of me.

I could never be this version of myself I once was, I value honesty and communication. I don't let anyone in my space who's a threat to me or my heart. It's possible to not make the same mistake twice, that's why unlearning is important.

Hidden Gems

You gotta be strong enough
to **stand in your truth**.
Once you do,
no one can break you.

Hidden Gems

Your opinion of me is just your opinion.
It doesn't validate me.
It doesn't change who I am.
It doesn't make a difference.
It just says a lot about you.

Hidden Gems

Don't stay because you're loyal,
walk away because you're loyal.
Don't keep giving
the best parts of you
to someone
who doesn't deserve them.

Hidden Gems

If you **push me away**,
I promise you
this will be the last.
I sacrificed myself
too many times,
to be your safe place.
I don't have what it takes
to keep bruising my soul
for your ego.

Hidden Gems

To build a home

out of you, I tried.
I only ended up homeless
Intertwined with momentums,
of my darkest hour
brought to light.

Hidden Gems

Talks with my heart

Do you ever wonder why you feel so broken after they leave you? It might be the fact you loved them very much, that you pictured this life with them that you invested all this time into them, and you never imagined you'd need to let them go. They were your person; your everything. You couldn't picture yourself with anyone else. You didn't want to picture anyone because they were the only ones. So, they left you, and that's why you feel broken. You always ignored the red flags because you were manipulated to believe they were more important than you were. You start to question, was this connection real, or was all in your head... this illusion of love you chased for so long you refuse to let go. That's why you feel broken. It's true, relationships do come to an end, and people leave... they move on and outgrow you. You aren't broken, you gave your all to someone in hopes they were going to return the same feeling to you and you feel broken because they didn't. You feel as if some way you both missed your path, that where you wanted to be isn't where wanted to travel. The love once there turned into pain and that's because you kept fighting for something that wasn't in the cards for you.

Hidden Gems

Heartbreak reflection

Someone once said, "you have love, you don't know what it's like to not have it" as if I didn't sacrifice my heart to once be loved. I didn't wake up one day and end up with this love… I spent a lot of years alone wondering if I would ever find the one. I spent a lot of years with the right ones for the moment but ended up wrong in the long run. They were stepping stones to this love I cherish. I was clingy when it came to the thought of love, I created it within everyone who made me feel something. I once chased and manipulated myself to believe I was somehow worthy of a love that was never good to me. I internalized a lot of what I believed was for me, until I could escape the pathetic love, I once depended on myself. We all have that one heartbreak we'll always remember.

Hidden Gems

A letter to a toxic love:

You were so good at faking, it made me wonder… what in my life was real? You gaslighted me so much, to the point I didn't know what I was feeling. The person I was, went to this place so dark I couldn't escape. The manipulation of making it look like it was me and it was you all along. You had me question my feelings, emotions, and intentions. You had me questioning whether I loved myself in the beginning, you were this wonderful person. You made it seem as if the chase for your love was a reward, the more I chased the more I'd get and all I received was a broken heart. I got trust issues and a constant voice in my head asking I'm wondering to ever find love again. Real love, not the love you made me believe was real. The saddest part is going into these new relationships and connections thinking I'm the one who isn't worthy, and I'm the one who has something to work on. I'm going into these relationships with my toxic traits from patterns you taught me, all because the love I thought lived within you was a love that was real. I probably turned down ones good for me so many times because I was used to choosing the wrong ones. After all, that fake love felt so real to me.

Hidden Gems

My need to rescue, my need to save, fix, and heal the broken- because that's just me in my element. I felt broken and the only way I felt whole was to save someone until I was faced with despair. I could only save myself, so once I left you behind there was a lot I needed to work on. I did that and I found love, real love, thanks to you.

Hidden Gems

Lessons in love:

A cold heart isn't a home,
don't waste your tenderness
trying to warm it.

Hidden Gems

Decluttering my heart-
evicting everyone
and everything
that doesn't bring my soul peace.

Hidden Gems

Trauma Bonded

I was searching for someone to save me, I put the burden on you, and everyone who passed through my heart. Our brokenness connected us; we were both searching to feel something.

Hidden Gems

Selenophile

Sharing the same love for the moon,

- *a love language*

Hidden Gems

My Moon

It's impossible to forget you, not saying I want to because I don't wish to, but sometimes, I try to remember you without the pain attached. I don't want the happiness surrounding you to ache with sorrow. I don't want the love I have for you to weaken. I don't want your memory to fade. I don't want what we had to be an afterthought… I want this grief to finally turn into peace.

Hidden Gems

Beauty in the darkness

The greatest heartbreak I ever felt was watching someone I love transition into the universe. Without a goodbye, without a moment to understand why. My heart, soul, and entire being were in chaos. I questioned my existence often. I questioned life. I questioned how I was going to move on without the love that brought a different feel, one I could never replace or re-feel. I felt if I did, it would be disrespectful to the connection we shared. I sat in misery. I cried myself to sleep. I couldn't breathe. I almost gave up trying to find purpose until they reassured me that I was the purpose. They made sure I knew I was worthy, and that my existence was needed.

Hidden Gems

Mirrors

Reflections always dig up the pain,
that's why the past is a dangerous place.
Don't go back if you don't think
it's something
you'd survive twice.

Soul-tied

I found peace in letting go and walking away from people who helped me see a version of myself I couldn't before. I was accustomed to their opinions and their version of me. I couldn't see through their reviews. I don't know why I let someone invest so much in me just so they could change me. I lost myself while loving a version of myself someone created. I loved someone who never truly knew me but somehow we were soul-tied- the bittersweet but never love the same way twice, soul-tied.

Hidden Gems

If my heart could talk:

I'm just fortunate to feel something.
As it whispers,
"I just want to feel nothing"

- *heartbreak paradox*

Hidden Gems

I never love the same way twice,
everyone got a different version of me.
Not everyone was lucky enough
to be gifted
the best parts of me.

Mirrors II

You'll never grow until you do a deep reflection on yourself and take accountability for the pain you brought to yourself and others. Pointing the finger at others is easy but the blame can only go so far until you become toxic from the habit of never owning up to your part.

Hidden Gems

The *one* true love is **you**,
never realizing that
will always make you feel broken.

Hidden Gems

Free Write

If you haven't in a while if you've been busy, reach out to someone you love and remind them you love them. That text or call will be enough to make them feel good- to know they were a passing thought through your chaos, will be enough. We get caught up in our lives and forget how important it is to reach out to our loved ones. Forever isn't within our reach, we live in the moment. Grudges may seem strong and it's up to you to hold onto them, but if you fell off with someone you love that can be rekindled- rebuilding a new bridge with the foundation you taught yourself is healthy for you. Sometimes we get caught up in ourselves, and our lives, and we don't realize sometimes we let people go who didn't deserve to be ghosted or burdened by our need to find ourselves. Sometimes the apology comes from you and it's needed. Sometimes you love someone but they don't need to be a part of your life.

Hidden Gems

Sometimes someone wrongs you but they were hurting too. To forgive and apologize is one thing. To have them in your life is completely different. One thing I learned through my journey is to be accountable- it's a level of growth where nothing negative can touch you if you're honest with yourself and your intentions. Always communicate- don't expect someone to read your mind. To keep a healthy relationship you need to do the work… but when you love someone it won't feel like work it will just make sense.

Hidden Gems

It doesn't matter how much support you receive; your loved ones should always support and celebrate you. Your big wins, the small ones too. They shouldn't be afraid to show and share it with you. No one who loves you will make you feel like you don't deserve happiness.

Hidden Gems

Livin' Outside My Comfort Zone

A lot of things make me uncomfortable. Simple-minded people make me uncomfortable. Being around people I don't know while being alone. Being forced to expose part of myself I'm not ready to, makes me uncomfortable. People who can't accept me for who I am. People who are comfortable bad-mouthing someone they love to me, make me uncomfortable. People who fake it for the sake of love for you, instead of communicating an issue, make me uncomfortable. People criticize someone for a story they don't know the complete version of or even a chapter of. Perfectionists make me uncomfortable, along with the judgments that follow. Being someone reserved and intuitive like me, I find comfort hard to come by, so when someone sparks peace within my soul, I always love them hard. Sometimes that makes me uncomfortable, too. It didn't always come from a healthy place. Finding the beauty in each uncomfortable moment was the peace I needed. I was able to be the healed version I always yearned to be.

Hidden Gems

Get out of the mindset that when someone leaves you, you gotta resort to who's to blame. Sometimes it's the universe redirecting you to a new path, yes it will sting for some time, and probably even ruin you until you see the silver lining. Not everything is meant to be.

Hidden Gems

The Inevitable

If there's one thing I learned in love, it's not to ever say, "I should have never loved them" because you were meant to, even if it doesn't feel like it, even if it didn't end up the love you longed for. The one thing we often get confused about is love, the idea we place upon those we love… the idea of this fantasy of two people being molded together in this wholehearted bliss. A connection that lasts forever and doesn't even exist. I feel we bask in the mirage we're infatuated with and once someone gives us an ounce of what felt like love, we give in and let our guard down. There's no manual when it comes to loving someone, you don't pick and choose who you fall for, sometimes it happens without warning, and it happens before someone falls in love with you too. Sometimes they don't fall for you, a least not the same way you want them to. We rarely talk about the treasure of loving someone on our own. We talk about how much we give, and how much of us is

Hidden Gems

unfinished but we choose them. We don't talk about how special it is to love someone even if they don't return it. The capacity of love we have to give and the hopelessness we always nurture back to life. We talk about how our heart breaks from the love not being reciprocated but we don't talk about maybe it just wasn't meant to be. We don't talk about how we try to fill a void we also hold in vain. We don't talk about victimizing ourselves while making them the monster, all because we loved harder, and they didn't love us at all. We don't talk about how we kept our hearts open, we kept investing when they were honest from the beginning. The number of times I indulged in love. The many times I was fooled by the butterflies. My moment of truth was when I realized my heart couldn't be broken because of the lack of love I received... it could only be broken by giving it to the mercy of those who didn't want it.

Hidden Gems

I'm thankful for the negative reminders, the negative mindsets, and the negative vibes that have come to take me down but failed terribly. Some may have caught me at my lowest, but none were able to break me. My negative thoughts have served me so much purpose- a redirection, a wake-up call to the path I'm destined for.

Hidden Gems

Platonic Heartbreak

One thing that hurts harder than any breakup is getting your heart broken by your best friend. Someone you invested so much love, respect, trust, and appreciation for. We don't talk about how best friend heartbreaks are one of the worst heartbreaks of all. When we think of a best friend, we think of someone who will be there until the end of time… someone you can call, or run to, especially when the times get dark, they're the lift and light you need. We spend many years heart and heart with our best friend. Unforgettable nights, endless memories, late-night talks, and crying sessions. Don't forget they're someone who never judges or belittles you. They listen, care, and comfort you. I know there are many souls out there who have this friendship and I wouldn't recommend letting it go, but it's time to talk about the side of friendship no one talks about and how it's not always an everlasting connection. There's no rule book when it comes to choosing your friends or anyone in your life. You choose these souls because

Hidden Gems

they choose you. they give you a safe place to open and that's what you latch to. We don't talk about how it's possible to one day outgrow them because our life gives us no choice. We don't talk about how one day they don't feel like they're our best friends anymore. We don't talk about how what once was a solid foundation turned into silent judgments and competition. We don't talk about how we see the change, but we make excuses just to keep them in our lives… hoping we can prevent our best friend from slipping away. No one tells you that it's impossible to keep someone in your life even after years or decades of love. No one tells you that it's okay to walk away, outgrow, and choose yourself when someone is no longer serving you. I always recommend holding on tight to any connection worth the effort, but I also believe in setting free those who I love even if it means I need to live without them. I no longer try to unlock the secret to why I need to leave them behind, I just trust it's all a part of a bigger picture. I choose to hold love for them forever, but ultimately, I choose growth.

Hidden Gems

Past reflections

One thing that lacked in my previous relationships was the ability to connect with my partners on an emotional level. None of them were open enough to speak their fears, feelings, or madness. Instead, they shut me out. Being someone whos an over-expressive, and emotional soul, I couldn't adapt. I'm too intuitive, I like to speak about how I feel, and it helps me get through any situation. I might need time to reflect but I never let the situation disappear without communicating it. My past was the opposite, I held so much in because of it. It's hard to love someone and not fully express that love. I became trapped in my mind to the point I cried more than anything because I was confused, I lost the ability to express myself being with someone so cold. To them, I was toxic because they didn't understand truly why I left they ran with their version of the story. To me, I detached from us because I couldn't connect or truly love because I wasn't appreciated for who I am.

Hidden Gems

A word of advice to anyone in a relationship with someone who doesn't care to hear you out or thinks you're overly emotional, don't stick around. It's not good for you to hold in everything you feel to make them satisfied, let them find someone as emotionless as them. Relationships include friendships and family, the label doesn't matter. Anyone in your life that can't communicate with you won't ever fully understand you or be what you need.

Hidden Gems

Too much pride
will make you feel
like you're on top of the world,
but will leave you empty in the end.

Hidden Gems

Don't set high expectations when it comes to second chances with someone who broke you. No matter how many times you try and rewrite it, some stories are meant to be cut short... and some end when they do.

Start a new story
with a new you,
one not attached to the past.

Hidden Gems

Note to self:

I hope you have the courage to plant tenderness in places you didn't think could exist, but with your presence, it blooms.

I hope you know the power you possess, the potential you hold… and the peace waiting for you.

I hope you know.

Reminiscing

I remember watching myself break into pieces watching the one I loved move on while I'm left trying to find the strength to set myself free of them. I remember the excruciating pain of watching the one I love, love someone else knowing that won't be me again. I remember them taking my heart for the same ride for the first time. That rush of lust that felt like love only leave my spirit crushed, only to leave me with all the things we had that are now the dust of memories in the shadow of us. I gave my all. I let my guard down. I proceeded with love only to be left trying to find peace in letting go. I wasn't ready to learn not everyone I loved would stay, I was too busy internalizing our forever.

Hidden Gems

I shouldn't have to dim my confidence in front of someone insecure. It took me a long time to be this confident and safe in my skin. Don't be so quick to judge when you don't know my journey.

- *Believing in myself saved me*

Hidden Gems

Adventures

I was once chasing the destination of love, happiness, and fulfillment and I came up short every time. I was craving a daydream. I desired a fantasy that was out of reach. I overlooked moments that were highlighted in front of me, red flags included, I decided to let disaster in just like I let love. I was chasing a destination all this time, thinking that one moment would be mine forever. One of the hardest lessons I learned, was life is not about the destination… it's not about where I'll end up, because there's always a pitstop and there will always be another destination. Most importantly, it's about each moment that led me to each destination… it's about the journey.

Hidden Gems

Giving yourself flowers before anyone else does is self-love. It's a boost of confidence. It's believing in your magic. Don't let anyone make you believe you need to wait to be cherished.

Hidden Gems

People that always go out of their way to express the negative and always place their energy on what doesn't serve them, aren't people I let close to me.

- *I know they'll never do right by me*

Hidden Gems

I masked the pain,
pretended to be okay.
The heartache was starting a fire in me
one I couldn't survive
I let it burn me slowly
with a smile on my face

- *I refused to let them win*

Hidden Gems

As liberating as it is
to let go,
It will still hurt.
The time and love invested
doesn't just disappear.

- *that doesn't mean stay*

Hidden Gems

Hallucinations

Maybe we found each other
at the wrong moment.
Maybe our forever
wasn't written in the clouds
and the stars didn't align for us.
Maybe our timing was off,
and we'll never pick up where we left off.
Maybe, just maybe
we were chasing a false reality.

Hidden Gems

I don't expect anyone I love to cater to my every need, especially when I'm going through it. No one can heal me, they can only stand by me and love me through every dark moment. I don't hold them to that, I understand we all go through it.

Hidden Gems

Far from home

Just because someone has become your safe place doesn't mean it's safe. Sometimes we become so invested that we don't see the red flags and sometimes we overlook them because of this feeling of sadness. Sometimes we latch to comfort because someone makes us feel something remotely different. Sometimes history with someone will have your heart locked in with no key to free you. The moment your intuition brings that wake-up call, believe it. Your body will tell you when something is wrong just as much as your mind and heart do. Dive deep into your soul. What is different this time from all the others? What is it that's keeping you? If the communication has flatlined and the feelings become one-sided, that's enough to walk away. The first instinct to go was when you questioned if you should. No one meant for you will ever have you running circles around them just to see if they love you.

Hidden Gems

The kind of chaos that comes from loving someone who makes you feel hard to love, they will forever have you searching for that love within them and anyone else before you find it within yourself. You deserve a love that doesn't make you feel the need to be a savior. The kind of love that doesn't make you check out on yourself just to check in on them. Reserve your love for those who don't use your heart as a weapon against you.

Hidden Gems

Searching for your safe place opens the door for comfort in ways not healthy for you. You accept them because you want to feel something. Someone being your safe place is more than feeling love, it's someone who doesn't make you question their intentions or love. It's someone you feel secure in their presence. It's someone who is honest and doesn't lie to you. It's someone who never makes you number two. You deserve a safe space to share your love with, someone who you find a home in. Before you find them, I hope you set a new foundation, and the right boundaries and build yourself a home, one that can't be taken from you. This time you won't allow strangers to create a safe place in you out of a trauma bond.

Hidden Gems

I can love you from afar
and set you free,
the cost of unconditional love
walking away
before I let you
consume me

Hidden Gems

I remember being someone
who wanted to find love,
I created love within people
who didn't have the potential
to love me,
not even half of what I gave.
I chose to love them.
I chose to give my heart.
I can't blame them
because I thought my love
would be enough.

Hidden Gems

Sometimes I prefer my own company
over being surrounded
by ones who adore me.
Sometimes I just need a break
from the world around me.
It's normal,
it's healthy,
and it's my therapy.

Hidden Gems

Love Notes

Hidden Gems

Hidden Gems

Lessons of love

I didn't need you to save me, that was my job, to save myself. We didn't meet in a broken moment; we were healed versions of ourselves. A healthy love could never be built on codependency.

Hidden Gems

Testimony

I didn't fall in love with you because of the idea of love I once created, I fell in love with you because you are the reason love bloomed in me. I had this idea of love for a long time that it was worth chasing and fighting for, but I chose to always go to war. I confused love with abuse. I lost track of the gift love truly is. I once had this idea of perfection, this idea of forever… neither exists in this world. It's the edge of imperfection that drives me, not someone who captures my heart just to leave it broken. Someone who loves me for the fact I'm not perfect. Someone who never forgets to remind me of the important things, but may occasionally forget the little things. Someone patient and always listens. Someone who takes care of my needs but gives me the space I need to breathe. I fell in love with you because of who you are first, not only how you make me feel.

Hidden Gems

My Person

I could not have loved you without being the healed version of myself- I mean, I could have, but I wouldn't know how to touch the parts of your heart you needed me to. I would be chasing empty souls, deserted in chaos to even take you seriously. The kind of love you gifted me was a wake-up call from the love I've been accepting for years. Your kind of love is the love I've been performing for years.

Versions of Love

My relationship taught me every relationship doesn't suffer ups and downs. It depends on the person you're with, what you haven't healed from, and what you're accepting. I'm not talking about mini arguments about little things because those times will come and they will be defeated. I'm talking about when someone doesn't communicate and it festers into more. I'm talking about when someone cheats instead of checking in with their partner. I'm talking about saying you're loyal but have no intentions of following through. Most of the time people get into new relationships without being healed from the last one, which causes a lot of friction in the new one. In my past every time someone treated me badly or even how I thought was deserving, I accepted it because I thought I had to fight for love as if it was a prize, I forgot what I was worthy of because I accepted less every time. People want to believe love is something you need to fight for, maybe because it leaves it with more depth. When you truly love someone, the healed version

Hidden Gems

of them, there's nothing you need to worry about. You need to be the healed version of yourself too. There won't be random arguments and trust issues or wondering when the relationship will break. It's possible to find someone who enhances your worth and loves you deeply without the pain attached. Don't settle for a love that's disguised as pain, a never-ending battle of heartache. Don't accept every offer of love that comes your way, not everyone will bring the best version of you out, find it within you first so you won't accept any version of someone.

Hidden Gems

Let's talk about love!

Does anyone talk about love and not just the heartbreak of never receiving it? I don't think we talk enough about the beauty of love and the essence of it. I see many people shame love as if love was the problem as if the wrong person and wrong time aren't a factor. I see many people blame love when their heart takes a turn for disaster, and they let themselves turn cold. I don't think we talk enough about how love isn't the reason you end up broken, it's trying to make someone love you back who isn't meant to. It's overindulging in a story that's outgrown you. it's fighting for someone who will never be good for you. Many people will fight but be unsure of what love is. No love will be out of touch to the point you need to chase and force it to be yours. A love that's real doesn't need to be convinced. Rough times arise but nothing close to abuse in any form. You should never fight for a love that's unhealthy and only destroys you. What once was love may turn into poison to you, some storylines aren't meant for the long run. A love for you will only protect you and keep you safe from ever feeling the same loneliness ever again.

Hidden Gems

Love is beautiful, patient, and kind. Love is something you feel that's honest, protecting, and surreal at the same time. Love is a feeling you feel when someone makes you feel warm, happy, and secure. It's time we talk about the love that is made for you, not the love you convinced yourself to believe was for you. It's time we talk about how love isn't something you fight for… it's something that will never make you question yourself or the place of someone you love. Some think this love is rare and that's because they accept love in all forms. It's time to open your eyes and protect yourself from the love you conditioned yourself to. It's time to free yourself from the dishonest hold you have on a love that only makes you believe it doesn't exist. Once you let go of any idea that love is at fault and the idea that you'll never find it, things will start aligning. Timing is everything, but it won't make something not meant for you right for you. Timing will only bring you two things: a lesson and a blessing, it's rare for both to be a part of the same story.

Hidden Gems

Sanctuary

I trusted you with my heart,
You introduced me to a different feel.
The kind of love
people make homes out of,
I found my sanctuary in you

Hidden Gems

Bonds

If someone made me feel, I embrace it. To me, it was inevitable, a moment that was meant for me. I had to. I couldn't overlook the tenderness when I felt it. I trusted it. It's rare, to ever touch my soul. It's rare, to capture my heart. Connections are something incredible.

Hidden Gems

<u>Honeymoon</u>

The honeymoon phase will never fade. Our love is intense and real, and I could never get tired of the affection or time you give me. Your warmth is the only love I want every day for the rest of my life. I've never dreamt of a future with anyone as I dream of ours.

Hidden Gems

July 10, 2022

It seems like yesterday we met and became friends, and not too long after became lovers. Today marks 4 years of us.
4 years of me falling more in love with you.

4 years of us growing and evolving into our best selves.

4 years of listening, guiding, and being the best other half to each other.

4 years of smiles, laughs, and many unforgettable memories.

4 years of inspiring and lifting each other.

These 4 years have been the greatest trip of my life, spending every moment with you. I knew from the moment we met I wanted to spend the rest of my life with you. It was more beautiful knowing the feeling was always mutual. I love you, I love us.

Hidden Gems

My soul craves a different kind of love and that's the kind of love you cater me with. The spontaneous, welcome-home kind of love. A love I never felt before. A love that's greater than any other kind of love I've experienced. Your love gives me security. Your love is special.

Hidden Gems

My heartbeat

One of my favorite moments was the moment you laid your head on my chest to intentionally listen to my heart. In that moment I knew how perfect you were, for me. For you to care to listen to how my heart beats for you, is something more beautiful than the words "I love you". In that moment it was racing because no one ever thought to listen. No one ever cared to know. You were the missing piece to my heart, and it knew. I knew there wasn't anyone who was more for me than you. There are so many moments I've taken with me but the best part is there are so many more to come. I'm so in love with you and where our future is headed. You have brought me so much light when it comes to what love is. I thank you for being someone rare in this world, for being the one I could fall in love with, letting me fall, and not forgetting to catch me.

Hidden Gems

I'd rather have everything with you
than to give any part of me
to anyone else.

Hidden Gems

Love drug

Your love taught me what love is supposed to feel like, not the assumption of what it's made out to be. You touched me with the kind of spark that leaves an imprint on the heart, the kind of love that can't be forgotten. Your light inspires the fire in me. your love makes me realize that no love I've consumed was ever good enough because you were the dose I needed.

Hidden Gems

Moon's Prayer

I thank you, for saving the love I deserved to give, for him. I thank you for making me wait for this love and letting me prepare myself enough to appreciate who I am, so I could embrace him. Learning to appreciate myself was a dark space I always ran from, but I accepted my heart is out of this world and that my beauty isn't only what people can see. I'm loving myself through my flaws. I know I was impatient, but it was brutal learning the importance of patience. I understand now, why you made me wait, nothing this breathtaking can be rushed. You prepared me for this love. I'm so thankful for the one you chose. I'm so thankful you chose the woman I am to be the woman he loves. I promise to protect him. Everything I've given, he's reciprocated. It's in my heart, to love him the way he deserves, to make sure he's always safe… because his heart is too delicate to break. If I could take my heart out and give it to him, I would, so he could feel every beat, the way it beats for him.

Hidden Gems

To my future husband

Falling in love with you was like falling in love with everything I was fearful of. Love was a scary roller coaster of emotions I never thought I was ready for when it came to giving parts of my heart no one deserved. I kept those parts in the dark, it wasn't until you, uncovered those parts. You opened my heart and my eyes to what I knew I deserved all along. You reciprocated those parts of my heart… you matched my heart with the love you shared. You inspired me. When it comes to our love, nothing will expire. Our passion is wild, our minds are in sync, and our hearts yearn as one. You made falling in love with myself feel as beautiful as falling in love with you. I don't know how I spent my whole life without you, but now that we're here, I promise loving me will be worth the ride.

Hidden Gems

I knew I loved you
the moment
I didn't fear you might leave.
Loving you
came naturally to me,
I wasn't afraid to embrace you.

Hidden Gems

Love Notes

The love I have for my partner is outta this world. The passion between us is wild. I couldn't give my heart to another, what we share is unique and it wouldn't feel right to love anyone else. That's how I know they're my person, my forever, and my souls match.

Hidden Gems

You are the finest
I've ever laid my eyes on
and so divine.
I never knew it was possible
to fall in love so many times
with one person,
over and over again.

Hidden Gems

My person is the most supportive, understanding, and unconditional lover. Truly blessed to have met someone so honest, warm-hearted, and beautiful. Every day, I wake up and realize I'm with a real-life angel, and how incredibly blessed to have someone who shares the same soul.

Hidden Gems

You look at me
like I'm the most beautiful woman
you ever laid eyes on.
You only search for me
in a crowded room.
The kind of energy
that forever gives me butterflies.

Hidden Gems

Falling in love with you is the most peaceful thing I experienced, in a whole full of chaos. Our worlds merged without fear, without doubt, and without pressure. Our love wasn't created overnight, it was before our time.

- *past life lovers*

Hidden Gems

I love having our place.
Cleaning our place.
Cooking our meals.
I love having a home to go to,
even though
everywhere with you
feels like home.

Hidden Gems

Heart 2 Hearts

I have someone who not only loves me as a lover, but I have "best friend moments" with. We're able to break into a heart-to-heart, honest reflection of ourselves without fear. That's why being in love with your best friend is lit.

Hidden Gems

Dedication

I promise to always love you, unconditionally. I promise to never let our flame burn out, but to only find new ways to love you. I know our love will make it through whatever life throws at us. We've both conquered loving ourselves, so loving each other is the easiest part.

Hidden Gems

Unforgettable Memories

As I played "so into you" by Tamia I had tears in my eyes watching him sing to me. Secure in his own skin, so pure. He didn't know the whole time I'm thinking how incredible to ever experience a love that's so unfamiliar to the outside world, a love that's only felt between us.

Hidden Gems

Do whatever it takes
to keep that spark alive,
the romance.
Don't get lazy
when it comes to loving someone
you don't want to live without.

Hidden Gems

If I had to choose my favorite thing about us, it would be our openness. Our communication and how we can talk for hours about anything and just vibe, and innerstand each other. That's how I know the foundation we've built can't be broken.

Hidden Gems

Someone who's soft
but not easily open,
I'm drawn to you.
You'll always be a mystery to me.
You'll always be someone
I want more from.
But for now,
know that being your friend
has been an honor.
I'm so happy
to call you my friend.
Knowing you
has been admired,
thanks for letting me in.

Hidden Gems

Falling in love with someone
you had no intention of falling for,
is the most beautiful kind of love.
No forcing chemistry,
or trying to save them.
Just a pure,
raw connection
created on its own.

Hidden Gems

For the first time in my life,
I'm not afraid to lose someone
because I know without a doubt,
our love can't be forgotten
or given to someone else.
Our souls can rest together.
Our souls found peace together.
Our souls found our hearts
and now they're home.

Hidden Gems

I genuinely fell for someone when I walked away from what no longer fed my soul. I left the baggage behind and they discovered me. They sparked my life with their light and made all the difference. I wasn't searching for them, I was pursuing peace. I was loving myself. Sometimes you just need to be patient and focus on you and the right ones will fall into your life and choose you.

Hidden Gems

Hidden Gems

We stay because we love hard. We put our hearts all in and there's no taking the love back. We manipulate our hearts to believe if we felt love, it was. We're taught to hold anyone close who made us feel something. When the same comfort they gave felt like home. We condition our hearts to believe we need their love since we've been dependent on it… we didn't once think it could be possible to live without it. We stay in hopes they change their heart and one day come back to us. We stay for the simple reason we love hard, making it hard to be loved in return knowing our worth is far more than what we're accepting… yet we consume less because we don't believe we're good enough.

Hidden Gems

You won't always get that apology you're owed. You won't always get the closure you need. You won't always be felt and understood when it comes to your feelings. How you feel is valid but sometimes people don't understand they hurt you even if the proof is right in front of them. They will deny it because they don't view it the same as you, and that's okay. You don't need an apology or closure from someone who can't admit to the pain they caused you. You will heal and grow regardless. Be patient, and embody how you feel because it's real. Don't let their manipulation change that.

Hidden Gems

"I love you because of your energy"
Is the most beautiful compliment
I've ever received.

Hidden Gems

Dreams do come true

I remember dreaming of being an author. I remember falling in love with writing way back. I'm so proud of myself for everything I've accomplished. I'm so happy I've found my place and purpose in this world. I'm so fortunate I found myself.

Hidden Gems

Thank you for always listening.
Thank you for giving my work a chance.

Hidden Gems

My **platforms**:

Instagram: Moonsoulchild
Twitter: Bymoonsoulchild
Tiktok: Bymoonsoulchild
Facebook: Moonsoulchild
Apple Music & Spotify: Moonsoulchild

Moonsoulchild.com

Hidden Gems

*All my **books**:*

The Journey Through My Heart
Vol. 1 and 2

I Was Never Broken
Vol. 1 and 2

Letters To You

Dear Anonymous

YoungNakedSoul

Heal Inspire Love
Self-Talks
(co-write with Michael Tavon)

Soul of Cancers

The Feels the Moon & My Soul
The Feels the Moon & My Soul
(Deluxe prompt version)

Hidden Gems

The Feelings and Healing Collection:

Finding self
Healthy Connections
Grief

Discovering
Twin Souls
Broken

Soulmates
Healing
Insecurities
Toxic Connections